The Pipe
and
the Pulpit

Dr. Basha P. Jordan, Jr., D.Min.

Contents

DEDICATION

To my wife Pia who has been a tremendous inspiration and my mother Doreatha (deceased) who always supported me and my children, Basha, III and Christina who inspire me to greatness.

Introduction

When Bill Clinton was elected president of the United States in 1992, he said that drugs were the number one problem in the United States. The drug and alcohol problem in America has become increasingly worse over the years. In every major city in America, more and more people die daily as a direct result of drugs or alcohol. The arrest records show that in Baltimore, Maryland, alone, approximately 85 percent of people in the prison system are there because of drug- or alcohol-related crimes. Additionally, young and old alike can be seen daily on street corners, selling and buying drugs and drinking alcohol from brown paper bags.

However, the majority of the drugs that are consumed in America are not bought and sold on the streets. They are distributed and purchased by middle- and upper-class citizens who live in condominiums; town houses; spacious, luxury apartments; and private homes in suburbia. Marijuana, heroin, cocaine, prescription drugs, and alcohol are abused by schoolteachers, firefighters, doctors, ministers, lawyers, judges, politicians, and others who suffer from the disease of addiction. What makes it so devastating is that many of them are ignorant of the fact that they are addicts because of the stereotypical image portrayed by the news media and in television shows and in the movies. It is a widespread belief that addicts and alcoholics are only uneducated, lower-class, skid-row individuals, not those who are professionals, upper-class and highly educated in our society.

I was a pastor for eleven years before I went into treatment for drug addiction, and I was ignorant of the fact that anyone can suffer from the disease of addiction. I thought that my education, social standing, religious affiliation, financial situation, and ministerial credentials exempted me from the stigma of addiction. Wrong! Wrong! Wrong! My lack of knowledge almost cost me my life, a beautiful family, and my career. I don't want anyone to have to experience the horrors of addiction because of a lack of knowledge about the disease. There is a way of recovery through proven spiritual principles.

It is my hope that this book not only gives hope to addicted persons and informs individuals, families, and communities about available help. I also hope the church will become educated about how twelve-step programs such as Alcoholics Anonymous, Narcotics Anonymous, Gamblers Anonymous, and Overeaters Anonymous save lives and families. There is much that can be done to give hope to all substance abusers no matter what their profession or faith. The church and the faith communities are in positions to change lives and empower people on God's behalf. It's time to take our heads out of the sand and address those who are suffering right under our noses, right next door, and in our own homes with the proper prescription of hope that has proved to be effective. Love, understanding, faith, and hope are what have worked for me to stay drug- and alcohol-free since October 13, 1988. These same spiritual principles will also work for anyone who is willing to try them with the help of others who care. Recovery and deliverance from active addiction does not happen in a vacuum. We need others to aid us to stay in active addiction, and we need others to help us to stay in recovery.

Read my true story and be blessed so you can be a blessing to others in the name of Jesus Christ. All names have been changed to maintain anonymity while delivering this message of hope to those who suffer from the disease of addiction and to family members who suffer because of their love for the addicted individual.

It is possible for entire families to recover together with the help of the church, twelve-step programs, and loving people in our lives. Please do not think because you may not be drinking or using drugs like your loved one or friend that you are not suffering. If you live with a practicing addict or alcoholic you love, you are affected by his or her suffering more than you know. It is also possible for you to be an enabler, helping the alcoholic to stay sick by giving the person money, lying for him or her, or allowing the individual to live rent-free in your house while continuing to abuse alcohol. There is helpful information in this book that will open your eyes and allow you to get help for yourself, even if your loved one decides to continue in the downward spiral of active addiction.

Let me make it clear that the disease of addiction is not confined to drugs and alcohol. One may become addicted to a person, place, or thing. An individual, no matter what his or her educational, social, or economic background, can become caught up in an addiction that can cause job loss, family disintegration, death, hospital institutionalization, or a prison sentence. Gambling, eating, working, shopping, and sex can become addictive, especially if the disease of addiction runs in your family. It's possible to be so set against a specific addiction because a family member was devastated by it that you develop an addiction in another area without realizing it. A shopping or work addiction may not seem all that bad to you. But without treatment, the results can be so devastating that the family is destroyed, or suicide becomes an option. All addictions have the potential for negative endings if not treated. But as I say at the end of every one of my Addiction Radio broadcasts, which has aired since 1992 (600 AM radio in Baltimore, Maryland, at 7:30 a.m. Saturdays), "And remember, no matter what's going on with you today, there is hope for you."

Chapter 1

Caught Up in Denial

It was a hot Sunday night, and I had been in church all day. We didn't have two worship services every Sunday, but on this particular day, we did, and I preached both services. Now it was about nine thirty, and my regular cocaine dealer could not be found. So I had to do the next best thing to get high that night. I drove around until I spotted a woman I'd seen in one of my circles. She said she knew where to score. She readily got into my late-model Mercedes 300D and gave directions to a low-rent apartment complex in west Baltimore. I knew I didn't belong there, but the cocaine had my mind on a search-and-seizure mission.

Being street-smart, I parked right in front of the entrance of the housing complex, left the blinkers on, and followed her. We went inside and got on the elevator. The stench, the dim lights, and the turtle-like pace of the elevator were nerve-racking. Finally, we arrived at the third floor. I followed my dope fiend guide to a partially opened door. As we entered, I noticed there were no lights. The reflection from the streetlights allowed us to find our way to an open door. She entered and greeted a thin, male drug dealer who was sitting on a bare mattress. My money was given in exchange for the precious, white cocaine powder. I left in a hurry, and she stayed with the half-dazed dealer, hoping to con him out of more than what he had bargained for.

Coming down on the elevator was a story in itself. I thought I was going to be able to reach the first floor without stopping, but the elevator stopped on the fifth floor. Two thuggish young men got on, one on either side of me. As the elevator began the long, slow ride down, I looked straight ahead and prayed that they wouldn't rob me. My appearance and persona said "Don't bother me if you know what's good for you." I was so glad when the doors opened on the first floor, and I was able to walk swiftly to my car to sample the coke. I wondered, *How could I lower myself to go where I went to get my drug of choice? The danger! The insanity! What is going on?*

Most drug addicts who enter recovery and get clean have hit a bottom, and everything begins to turn sour. I was hitting mine, and it was coming fast after I started smoking cocaine. I could blame my frat brother Mo for introducing me to cocaine. He is dead now as a result of drugs and alcohol, which also destroyed his marriage and family. But blaming him would be an excuse. I chose to smoke the pipe when it was offered because I wanted to experience what others were feeling. I got the tremendous rush that was good in the beginning but so devastating in the end. It almost cost me my life.

Before going into treatment for twenty-eight days in Bel Air, Maryland, on Friday, October 13, 1988, I wanted to die. I thought there was no other way to escape active drug addiction than to take my life. So I put myself in death-defying situations, hoping and praying that God would take me from my daily misery of using drugs. But death would not come. Why not?

There is something worse than death. There is an experience available to some who go against God's will that is more horrible than dying. If God is not finished with you and knows that He can still get the glory out of your life, He will not let you die. The experience I refer to is wanting to die but being unable to. You believe there is no reason to live, but God knows what you don't; He is working on your character through active addiction. All you know is that it's living torment! You don't know why He's doing this, because you can't see it.

God knows and cares about you more than you care about yourself. He's got your back, even when you can't begin to fathom what is happening. He's preparing you to do something for Him. As Tamela Mann sings, "He's got a master plan." It's called destiny, and you are totally oblivious to the spiritual metamorphosis being executed by the Supreme Power of the universe without your permission. He operates on your mind, body, soul, and spirit. In our weaknesses, God makes us strong, keeping us in His hands. We just don't realize it. When I'm thinking, *He's abandoned me,* He is with me more than ever. God will carry us when we are not qualified to carry ourselves. There's hope in the middle of dope.

Now, twenty-seven years later, I know what I didn't know before. I know God cares for me when I don't care for myself. When I don't know what, why, when, or how, He knows more about me than I know about myself. Why? Because He made me for His purpose and wants me to do what He created me to do. Now I know why He wouldn't let me die; He had something greater in store for me. His plan for me from my mother's womb is to give hope to those who feel hopeless. His plan for me is to let the world know that He is able to do abundantly above all that we can ask or think. The Master can do this even when we abuse alcohol, drugs, people, or things. If you are still alive, God is still working on you. Death is the final curtain, drawn only by the hand of God when all possibilities of us doing more for Him are over.

I now know beyond a shadow of a doubt that if God delivered me from thirty years of active drug addiction, He can do it for you without your permission. Just because you may want to throw in the towel, maybe, just maybe, the God of your understanding is training you for a higher calling than you can imagine right now. But you will understand it bye and bye—if you live. That's why I travel; preach; plan addiction conferences; counsel; attend twelve-step meetings; minister to convicts, politicians, doctors, and ministers; have radio broadcasts; and serve others who suffer. I do it because God molded me in the fiery oven of active addiction and brought me out to be His living example of hope. Having faith is the bottom line of believing you will come out of the pit. The invisible is more powerful than the visible. When we are caught up in denial, we don't know what's going on until we come out of denial. If we follow the Spirit's unction and choose life, we will come out of denial into the reality of what our life is really about.

My story is told to give you hope, especially if you are in active addiction or know someone who is struggling with addiction and you hurt for them. You may weep now in the midnight of your struggle, but joy will come in the morning if you have faith to believe it will. If you are suicidal, like I was, wait until tomorrow, and see what God has in store for you. Morning may come sooner than you think. My morning has come, and the sun is brightly shinning. As a matter of fact, the joy I have now cannot compare to the misery and pain of active addiction. Read my story with an air of expectation for a miracle to take place in your life like it has in mine. Make sure to interpret what's being said between the lines carefully because there is spiritual revelation that only the keen observer will grasp. I have prayed that revelation knowledge will be imparted to you as you read.

Looking back now, I realize I was caught up in a grip and could not help myself. Not knowing that I suffered from the disease of addiction, like many of my family members, caused me to get involved in many terrifying situations. Now I realize that the problem is a disease that can strike anyone in any profession and any economic status. This does not make me a bad person as I once thought. I suffer from an illness that needs proper attention. God puts people in our lives to help us when we are unable to help ourselves. Some addicts have been able to quit by just stopping or because of a spiritual awakening by going to church. This way is possible but highly unusual. However, until a person's mind is made up to find another way of living and follow a daily, spiritual program of recovery, the ends are always the same: jails, institutions, or death. The information and experiential wisdom transmitted to you through this writing gives you the opportunity to choose life for yourself and others you love.

Chapter 2

Cigarettes: My Gateway Drug

The earliest memory I have of using a mind-altering chemical began when I was about ten years old. My father, a Methodist preacher of forty-four years, smoked cigarettes. He would buy a carton of cigarettes, take a homemade butcher knife, and cut the whole carton in half, lengthwise. Instead of having twenty smokes per pack, he had forty. Daddy kept them in a drawer beside the bed.

Ever since I could remember, my father, Reverend Basha P. Jordan Sr., smoked a cigarette with a black and silver cigarette holder he kept in his vest pocket. He always wore a three-piece suit with a white shirt and tie. Daddy wore high-top shoes and a hat to match his outfit. My father was a neat dresser all the time. That cigarette, which burned slowly in his silver holder, seemed to mesmerize me. Daddy looked so sharp that I had to imitate him, even his cigarette smoking. Little did I know that this was the beginning of a life of substance abuse.

When my father wasn't looking, I would take a cigarette from his open pack on the nightstand next to his bed. They were easily accessible to this little, confused child who was being greatly negatively influenced by his father and didn't even know it. How many parents are leaving cigarettes, illegal drugs, alcohol, and prescription drugs open to children who are using them like I was. My father didn't have a clue about the addiction-and cancer-causing nicotine and other agents inherent in cigarettes. He was an innocent enabler for me to be "off to the races" with my disease of addiction. Off to the races, means a person's addiction is starting and happening without the knowledge of the individual who uses the drug. Addiction can manifest itself in other areas of an individual's life. It is obsessive, compulsive behavior, and the person who exhibits this behavior often doesn't know it exists until it is out of control.

I'd take the cigarette into the bathroom, lean out the window, and smoke it just like Dad. Little did I know that the nicotine was having an effect on me that would last thirty years. No one knew back then about addiction in our community, and the surgeon general had not yet put a warning on a pack of cigarettes about smoking causing cancer. Usually only men smoked openly. Nobody said anything about my father, the preacher, smoking cigarettes. Maybe he also carried a message to others that it was all right to smoke because ministers were very well respected throughout our community, especially in the late 1950s when I began smoking cigarettes. Daddy smoked Chesterfields and Pall Mall cigarettes. There were no filters on cigarettes then, and when I inhaled, a tremendous rush went through my entire body.

Once, I was in the bathroom on the second floor, leaning out the window smoking a cigarette. We were living in Laytonsville, Maryland, at the time, in a rural community. One of our neighbors, Mr. Green, raised hogs, and they used to get out of their pens a lot. On this particular day, a couple of the hogs were going through our trash cans, which were right below the window where I was smoking. As I leaned out the window, I flicked the ashes, and they fell on the backs of the hogs. I nearly fell out of the window due to the rush from the smoke. However, that didn't stop me from smoking Daddy's cigarettes. As I got older, smoking cigarettes became a favorite pastime and a vital part of my life for some twenty-five years. The only time that I didn't smoke was while I was active in sports all through school. But I did smoke during the off-season.

Cigarettes are addictive due to the drug nicotine, which is in tobacco. My father ended up dying as a direct result of smoking cigarettes. Emphysema attacked his lungs very badly later in life. He was hospitalized in his early eighties and was told to quit smoking. He stopped smoking for a short period after being released from the hospital. The next thing we knew, he discovered Carlton cigarettes, which were advertised to have low nicotine. He smoked these cigarettes until he died at the age of ninety. He was addicted to cigarettes, which took his life after a stroke. Even though I smoked cigarettes at the time of his death, I was more concerned about my father's health than my own because he had emphysema. My addiction had taken the focus off of myself and put it on my father.. This is the nature of the disease of addiction. The disease of addiction will trick you just like the Devil tricked Eve into eating the forbidden fruit in the Garden of Eden. The disease of addiction wants our lives, period.

Chapter 3

For Mama and Daddy

Cigarettes open the door for young people by making them feel more comfortable flirting with other drugs that are potentially more harmful than cigarettes. The body becomes accustomed to the feel, the "thrill" of smoking a cigarette and the whole mystique of smoking. Parents, please be careful how you deal with any drug around your children. They mimic us and want to be like us, no matter if the behavior is positive or negative. It is much easier for a person to smoke marijuana if he or she is already used to the world of cigarettes. The process of rolling, lighting, holding, inhaling, and blowing smoke is the same for both. Drugs that can be smoked are a danger to the life and welfare of the smoker. Fires, strokes, emphysema, and cancer are all killers related to smoking a drug. We do not want to influence our children to participate in habits that are not only addictive but that can cut life short as well.

Addiction destroyed many of my friends' and acquaintances' lives. My prayer is that the information shared here may prevent premature deaths, incarceration, maiming, and destruction of our communities and families. I have met addicts who have not only gotten high with their parents, but I know adults who have purchased drugs from their own children. I have had guests on my recovery radio broadcast who were made to wait in line in an alley while their grandson sold other addicts crack and then they purchased dope from their grandchild. This is insanity, but it is real. Parents are to raise children in the right way. Being caught up in the throes of drug addiction causes life to be lived in reverse gear. Here the child has the parent trained in the way he or she should not go.

I met one woman who sold drugs for her son. When she messed up his drug money because she, "shot the dope herself," he paid another addict to beat her up while he watched and spat on her. Her son was raised by his mother in a crack house where she prostituted herself in front of her children. Her son grew to hate her because of her neglect; her drug habit came before her children. Her son grew up to be just like his mother. Thank God she is in recovery today and has a master's degree. Unfortunately, her son is in prison for distribution of drugs. Parents need to set positive examples for their children, or they may end up in jail, institutionalized, or dead. Fathers are to be the spiritual heads of the home, showing their children positive ways earn a living and being present to show love to all at home.

There is another valuable lesson I have learned: "You can take a horse to water, but you can't make him drink." What does this have to do with addiction, drugs, and children? Well, I raised horses for twenty-five years, and my first horse taught me something I'll never forget. It was a hot day in the summer of 1989, and I'd been riding my thoroughbred, Cosmelia. She was sweating, and I knew she wanted a drink of water. I led her over to the water tub and told her to drink. She weighed about fourteen hundred pounds and just stood there, looking at me. I tried to pull her head down into the water tub with the lead line connected to her halter around her head, but she resisted. Out of frustration because this horse wouldn't do what I wanted her to do, I yanked the lead line down hard. For your information, I found out later that the strongest part of a horse is the neck. At that moment, Cosmelia threw her head up and backed up at the same time with such force that I was raised off my feet and almost knocked down. I was ticked off, but I knew that if I continued to try to force her to drink, I would get hurt. I decided to let her alone. Cosmelia came back and drank later in the day when she was thirsty, not when I thought she was thirsty.

We can tell our children about the negative arenas of life and see to it that they get as much education as possible in this area. We can pray and ask God to keep them off alcohol and shout all we want when we find evidence they smoke weed or something else. However, believe this. Our children are not going to always do what we want them to do. We have to allow them to decide for themselves when to do what we have suggested. When they get thirsty enough or are in enough pain, that's when they'll respond—if ever. People who are not ready for recovery will hurt you if you try to force them before they are truly thirsty for what is good for them. In the meantime, keep them in prayer, and let God handle them. He handled us, didn't He?

In raising my son and daughter, I shared with them many times about my struggles with addiction. After having discussions, taking them to twelve-step meetings and leading by example, I had to leave it to my Higher Power and them to make their own choices. Studies have shown that addiction is a family disease, and some family members are more prone to it than others. Some family members are in denial about the subtle grip addiction can have. I've learned that children do not always do what parents think they will. If you don't believe it, just remember what you did when you were their age. I forgot I did not do what my parents wanted me to do when they wanted me to do it. I only began to do what was right after much pain and after *I* decided that I was thirsty.

Prayer and pain are both motivating factors that will work for mama and daddy. Just be there for your children, no matter what. I messed up many times growing up, but thank God for a faithful mother and father who were there when I needed them. It will work for you, too, especially if you let go and let God. And what's so good about this tactic is when He works, nobody can get Him back. He will save us from ourselves and our children when we don't have a clue about what to do!

Chapter 4

That First Drink

Peer pressure is tremendous, and the idea of wanting to be accepted can take us into arenas that are not so easy to escape. Had I known what was going to happen as a direct result of taking that first drink, I would have said no thanks and walked away. However, wanting to be liked by others and having an intense inner yearning for excitement and acceptance, it was easy for me to stray from the righteous path on which my parents raised me.

There was no alcohol in my father's house except for a home remedy he made to ward off illness. The remedy consisted of fresh lemons, Anacin tablets, alum, asafetida tablets, honey, vodka or gin, and whiskey mixed together and stirred in a big pot on the kitchen stove. As children, Daddy would give us a tablespoon of the remedy anytime he thought we were getting sick. He would keep a bottle of the mix next to his bed and take a dose on a regular basis. It must have done the job because I never saw him sick or in the hospital until he had emphysema in his eighties. My sister and I were never in the hospital and rarely even got a cold while living in my father's house. I will probably mix up this remedy in my older years. There is longevity in my family on both my mother's and father's sides of the family. My father died at the age of ninety in 1980, and my mom died at age eighty-nine in 2013. My uncle Elder died in 1980 at age ninety-four. My paternal grandmother was a full-blooded Cherokee who went out in the woods and dug up roots for medicinal purposes for the family.

It was on a Sunday morning in 1960. My father was the pastor of Centennial United Methodist Church in Baltimore, Maryland, preaching at the 11 a.m. worship hour. For some reason, I walked outside when I should have been in church and saw a few young men sitting on the steps on Stirling Street. They were drinking Thunderbird, a cheap wine, with orange juice. One of them hollered at me, "Hey, preacher boy. Come here." Since the man who called me had a lot of influence in the neighborhood, I went over to the steps and was presented with the opportunity to take my first taste of alcohol. I didn't want to offend them and desired to be accepted. He invited me inside where everyone sat down, except me. He poured me a half glass of wine and chased it with some cold orange juice. As I stood there in my black, Sunday suit at the age of thirteen, surrounded by these men, I lifted the glass to my lips and drank some. Even though it tasted good and bad at the same time, I wanted to get back inside the church before I was missed. The warm feeling that came over me was the beginning of a rough journey that started with only a flicker of an alcohol flame and took twenty-five years to put out.

The seemingly innocent taste of that one drink of Thunderbird began twenty-five years of chasing a drink at every party, social gathering, and private celebration. Thank God my drinking didn't take off until after I stopped playing sports in school. When I went to Morgan State University and stopped playing football, I joined a military fraternity, the Pershing Rifles. Drinking became a favorite pastime for me, especially on the weekends. I was innocent and ignorant of the facts underlying the hidden struggles of countless members of my family with cigarettes, alcohol, and other drugs. Years later I found out that drug and alcohol addiction is on both sides of my family. It's amazing what we can find out about our families after we get caught up in a vice too tight to get out of alone—if we ask.

The first time I got drunk was at a house party during my first semester at Morgan. I was seventeen and big enough to buy alcohol without having to produce an identification card. It was on a Friday night at my buddy William's house (who died in the 1980s). We lived in Morgan Park about two blocks from each other, near Morgan State University. There was enough snow on the ground to hide the half-pint of Smirnoff vodka until I felt it was the right time to drink it, alone. The music was jumping, the strobe lights were blinking, and the party was a little crowded. It was about 9:30 p.m., and I figured I had to get a buzz going early because I had to be home around 11 p.m. This was the first house party that my parents allowed me to attend. I went outside, found the ice-cold bottle, and drank it down. It took me all of about five minutes to consume the entire bottle. Little did I know drinking that much alcohol that quickly would be a disaster. I walked back into the party, and within about ten minutes, I was drunk and didn't know it.

The long, black, mohair sweater I had worn became too hot while I was dancing the jitterbug. When the slow record started playing, I finally found a girl to dance with me, and while I was dancing, it became very difficult to stand. Then the unthinkable happened. Someone called me by my nickname: "Duke, come upstairs." I stumbled upstairs to see none other than my mother, sitting on the living room couch. Mama had come to check on her son because it was getting late. The shock and embarrassment were magnified because I was drunk. My mother was flabbergasted and disappointed. She escorted me out of the party, ignoring my feeble attempt to stay. Some of my friends were upstairs to witness this memorable event. Thank God Mama didn't tell my father. He was asleep by the time we walked the two blocks home. Whoever said that vodka doesn't smell on your breath lied. Mama smelled it right away.

My best friend, who had the party, started drinking regularly in high school. I remember trying to get him to slow down on his alcohol consumption. I didn't realize it then, but he was an alcoholic, and so was his brother. My drinking increased during our close friendship. I ended up in recovery, but he died a horrible death as a direct result of alcoholism. He was on his way home from work and was robbed after being hit in the head with a pipe. During the emergency hospital visit, it was found out that alcohol had deteriorated vital organs of his body. In order to get him to stop drinking, his mouth was wired shut.

On finding out about his condition, I visited him to pray for and console him. While sitting at the kitchen table, I noticed he had a McDonald's cup with a straw. After sitting there for a while, I began to smell alcohol, which he had mixed with the orange soda in the cup. This hurt me to my heart. I realized that I could not make him stop drinking even though it was killing him. He told me that he was going to die anyway so let him die in peace. I prayed, talked to his mother, whom I loved dearly, and left thinking that he was the only one who had the drinking problem. My drinking problem had not yet revealed itself to me. I was in deep denial. My best friend died about two weeks later.

Alcohol is the most misused drug in America, next to food according to Dr. James Dail, a noted wholistic theologian and author, minister of health. What makes alcohol so cunning is that it is legal. Most people do not even consider it a drug until it has destroyed the family, the job, the mind, and the spirit. My best friend was one of the most intelligent people I have ever met. He held some of the most prestigious and high-salaried jobs available in Fortune 500 companies. He was vice president of one or two of these companies and would talk about those "martini lunches" where many deals were made over alcohol. Many Americans of all races have fallen into the martini lunch trap, which allows alcoholics to be made, sustained, and in denial for years. If you know of someone who regularly drinks at lunchtime with clients, making deals and getting intoxicated, let them know of your concern. Have the person consult a physician or discuss with him or her the possibility of being addicted to alcohol. Send the person to the Alcoholics Anonymous website to take the test for alcoholism. Your confrontation could save a life. It could be your life and the lives of your family members. Drinking and driving kills thousands of people every year, and many of them are innocent victims who never saw it coming. Give a friend or loved one some hope by saying something before it's too late.

Chapter 5

Marijuana: The First Joint

By the time I was in my sophomore year at Morgan, the party scene was a regular weekend adventure for me. Bacardi rum and Coke was the popular drink for males and females. Beer and light wine were everywhere on and off campus, especially at the parties thrown by the fraternities and sororities. The Kappas, Omega Psi Phi, and the Pershing Rifles were the most popular fraternities on campus, and I was strongly considering one of them at this time. It was believed women really flocked to you if you were a member of one of the frats.

One weekend the Alphas were giving a party in the heart of Baltimore. It was Friday night. I was driving my 1957 Chevy and had a couple of buddies with me as we went to the party. We picked up a bottle of Old Grand Dad and some beer on the way to get our heads feeling good. The place was packed, the music was jumping, and the women were everywhere. The DJ was spinning 45s by The Temptations, The Four Tops, and Al Green.

After a while, I had to go to the john to relieve myself of the alcohol consumed. As I stood at the urinal, two brothers entered the restroom and locked the door. I wondered what was going on and looked over my shoulder just to be safe. I had heard about reefer but hadn't really been interested in it. It was supposed to take you to another level of high; I really was cautious about going there. I had smelled it on campus and seen others smoke it from afar, but now it was up close. For real! As I walked toward the sink to wash my hands, I casually observed these two brothers light a joint and inhale. As one brother took a puff, he handed the joint to me, and I took it without hesitation. Had I not been a cigarette smoker, it would not have been so easy for me to smoke that first joint, inhale, hold it, and then exhale with almost no smoke coming out. All my Christian upbringing went out the window for sixty seconds. That's all the time it took for me to take that drug, which would become my friend for more than twenty-five years. I could have said no, but I didn't because my addiction had already taken off without my permission.

Drug addiction will slow walk you and sneak up on you like a thief in the night. Before you know it, you've got a habit. You end up chasing that first high for years but to no avail.

Now my disease had three drugs from which to choose—cigarettes, alcohol, and marijuana—and I was a willing participant. I was off to the races. If I had known then what I know now, I would have made a different choice and said, "No thanks," and kept walking. If I had said no, my life would have taken another path, but I believe this was in God's plan for me. The experiences I have had as a result of taking that first hit off that joint have allowed me to know some things I can share with others to give them hope. Many have died who followed the same path, but only by the grace and mercy of God am I alive to write about it. My deliverance is not taken for granted. Those who do end up returning to active addiction, and many never return. Remember that before you try the first one. If you don't pick it up, it won't get in you. These are simple yet profound words.

Marijuana became a staple item for me, like wearing shoes and a hat. Where I went, marijuana went. Whether I was smoking it, selling it, or trying to cop it in New York's Greenwich Village, reefer had me caught in a vicious cycle of getting, using, and finding ways and means to get more. I remember being with a group of professionals one evening in a high-rise luxury apartment, getting high off some extremely potent marijuana. As we sat in a friend's swanky living room, the news was on television about a tremendous bust of marijuana on a ship in the inner Harbor of Baltimore. I commented about wondering what happened to all the reefer the police confiscated, and my friend, who was a judge, replied, "Where do you think this came from that we are smoking." Make no mistake about it; marijuana makes the rounds through every community and economic strata in America.

Right then I knew there was truly addiction among those who had sworn to uphold the law. Even though the news report stated that the marijuana found on that ship had been destroyed through burning, all of it was not destroyed. Some of it was being burned and smoked right at the table where we were sitting. Marijuana is accepted among certain classes of people as a mild, mind-relaxing, social drug, almost like a fine wine. Today it is smoked openly on street corners, in moving automobiles, public restrooms, outdoor sporting events, and wedding receptions. There are even those like former Baltimore mayor

Kirk Smoke who have advocated that it become legalized and treated as a health issue. In some cities in America, marijuana may be purchased legally to treat certain ailments like glaucoma. However, the majority of the reefer smoked in the United States is not for medicinal purposes but for getting high to change one's mood.

Marijuana has caused great havoc in the lives of countless individuals because of its addictive qualities. It also is popularly known as a gateway drug because so many people have gone on to stronger drugs after becoming addicted to it first. It is sold by street corner hustlers, middle-class professionals, and international smugglers. Marijuana is big business in America and is valued and abused by those you might not expect.

In 2001 I opened a men's recovery house in Baltimore called The House of Hope. It is located next to the church I founded, Hope Alive Ministry Deliverance Fellowship. A few young men who have come through the house have only used marijuana. They were sent to the house through a state-sponsored program called Drug Court, which offered an alternative to serving time behind bars by completing our recovery program. Even though it led to their arrests, some of these men could not believe marijuana was addictive and caused problems in their lives. Some in our society believe that if they don't use heroin, cocaine, or other drugs, they do not have a problem. One young man who fit this description left the program early, relapsed on reefer, and ended up dead as a direct result of his marijuana induced behavior. This drug can cause one to act and react in ways that are unacceptable. Please do not be confused about this. Marijuana is an addictive drug that can alter the mind and cause people to be comfortable in an atmosphere of criminal behavior. One can be injured or killed by being involved in the lifestyle of getting, selling, and using of drugs even if that person is not using the drug.

Many Americans who smoke marijuana also use other illegal drugs which can put you in situations where violence occurs . There have been many incidents where persons were killed or injured because they were in the wrong place at the wrong time. Even though marijuana is used in some places for medical reasons, this does not eliminate the possibility of the criminal element being present .

Proper education in the area of drugs is essential for all ages and families. Besides using drugs, you can become caught up in addictive behavior through selling drugs and the fast acquisition of large sums of money. The show and tell of expensive cars, clothing, jewelry, and other material things, especially in the inner city, tend to captivate young minds and lure them away from the fundamentals of life. Education, self-respect, wisdom, and understanding often take a backseat when fast money and glamor are easier to obtain. Someone has to take the time to train and be a proper role model for our children if God's people are to be spared to live full lives as designed by the Creator. This requires sacrifice, solid core values, and discipline on the part of spiritual fathers and mothers who will not abandon children's. The needy are not just in the inner cities but in every crevice of our communities, whether in the city, county, or parish. Hope is needed everywhere!

Chapter 6

Will a Cop Smoke Dope?

It must have been around 1973 when my road partner, Mo, and I were on our way to New York to buy some wholesale clothes for my store on Charles Street. I was driving a late-model Cadillac, a Coupe de Ville, as we traveled up Interstate 95. We had an ounce of reefer and some hash, which we were smoking while listening to the latest tunes on the radio. As we were passing a joint back and forth, I looked to my left, and there was a state police car right beside us. The trooper pointed to me, motioning for me to pull over. The windows were up, and I told Mo to get rid of the reefer as I lowered the windows to let the marijuana smell out of the car.

As soon as I pulled over, I got out of the car and walked toward the state trooper's car to give my partner time to hide the evidence. The trooper stepped out of his car and asked, "What were you all doing in the car? You weren't smoking marijuana, were you?"

I lied. "Of course not, officer." He told me to open the trunk, and when I did, he readily smelled the marijuana and searched the trunk, finding nothing. As he approached the passenger side of my car, my friend never saw him coming because he was stoned. When the trooper opened the door, Mo almost fell out of the car. It didn't take long before the officer found the ounce of marijuana right under the armrest.

I immediately got humble. I knew he could lock us up, take the few thousand dollars we had in our pockets, and totally destroy our plans. I asked to speak with him privately as we went back and sat in his car. I showed him my picture ID and told him how I was a hardworking man and an upstanding citizen. Would he be so kind as to let us go because our families needed us, and I needed to keep my job? As we sat there, another trooper passed us on the opposite side of the highway, and I knew he would be back in a matter of minutes. "Sir, your buddy is coming over here. I want you to know that the reefer in that bag is powerful, and whoever smokes it doesn't need much. Why don't you take it, do what you want with it, and let us go? Please, officer?"

Well, he took the bag of marijuana, folded it up real tight, put it behind the sun visor, and said, "I'll have to give you a ticket to justify me stopping you."

I replied, "Officer, couldn't you just give me a warning ticket because I can't afford to get another ticket?"

He said, "All right," just as the other state trooper pulled up behind us. I took the warning notice, got in my car, and drove off, wondering who was going to get high off our stuff. Mo was shocked but believed I had some kind of connection with The Man upstairs. Now I believe God's favor was brought about by the prayers of my parents. This goes to show you that marijuana use is widespread, even among those who lock others up for smoking it.

The disease of addiction and the illegal use of drugs is among all classes of people. We were all upstanding citizens—a preacher, a fireman, and a judge—that night in the high-rise apartment, smoking illegal herb. We had fine careers and were well respected in the community. Don't be fooled like I was and believe that just because a person has a good job, lives in a nice home, has a good education, or is a state trooper he or she doesn't use drugs. This lie, straight from the Devil's mouth, has helped to destroy untold numbers of lives and is still doing so today. It's time to put the Devil under our feet and declare the truth about addiction. It has no respect of persons. Anyone can be destroyed by the lack of knowledge about the tremendous power of mind-altering chemicals, just as I was. Don't think it can't happen to you because you are so smart, have a degree from an Ivy League school, make six figures, and live on Knob Hill.

When I was working with the police in the Lexington Community of Baltimore city in the early 90's, I had the opportunity of talking with the Major of the Western District Police Department. He shared with me thatthere are more drugs used among the middle and upper class than the lower class. Drug and alcohol usage in America among the well-to-do makes street drug sales look like kindergarten. This was an eye opening statement to me coming from one who worked in this arena on a daily basis.

Chapter 7

Preacher's Kid Gone Wild

Who we are and what we do have a lot to do with the way we were raised and what we experienced as children. Being the son of a preacher and raised in the church were rather difficult. Minister's children are always expected to do the right thing and say the right words all the time because this was a reflection on the parents. My sister, Mary, and I were showcased in almost every arena of the church. We sang together as a duet in the morning services, on the radio broadcast, and when Daddy went out to preach at other churches. We were involved in the children's usher board, the choir, Sunday school, vacation Bible school, youth ministry and went with our parents on weekends to various conferences and workshops. Mary and I were complete opposites. She was the perfect child at home, in school, and everywhere else. I was drawn toward excitement or made things happen, especially when my father wasn't looking or was away from home.

Many of the church people I witnessed as a child were quick to judge others when they were living hypocritical lives and putting on a front on Sunday mornings for other people. My parents, however, taught us spiritual principles, and they lived them on a daily basis. I've never heard my father or mother say anything stronger than "shucks" when they became angry or upset. Yet there seemed to be something inside me that urged me to be rebellious and take chances to find out what it felt like to disobey my parents. Hence, I got whippings or other forms of punishment on a regular basis—when I got caught. So much of my time was spent being good that I wanted to experience the pleasures of being bad, and that's what I did as often as possible. It's called the lust of the flesh, which, if not overcome, will ruin

As I look back over my life, it took reading the basic textbook of a twelve-step program and working the steps with a sponsor to learn about myself. By getting help, I began to see that I was practicing addict behavior way before that first drink or drug. My wants and desires were the most important things in my life, and I was willing to go to any length to satisfy them. It's called "self-will run riot, according to the basic textbook of Narcotics Anonymous.." This preacher's kid had gone wild because of addiction, which was in me a long time before it was diagnosed. It runs in the family like other inherited traits. Addiction may skip a generation but will surface down the line in somebody in the family.

Addiction affects every area of our lives; it affects us physically, mentally, emotionally, and spiritually. The physical aspect of the disease is the obsessive-compulsive use of mind-altering chemicals and the inability to stop once started. The mental aspect is the overpowering desire to use even when we know we're killing ourselves. The spiritual part is the total self-centeredness. We think that we can stop anytime we want, but all evidence shows the contrary. Many are dying today because of the trickiness of the disease of addiction.

No matter how many times I was whipped or slapped by my father, in private and public, I wanted what I wanted and got it most of the time—despite the consequences. Many times my daddy sent me out to pick a switch, which he used to punish me. The switch had to be pliable and not break easily.

Sometimes it was his leather belt that he would take off to do the punishing. At times, welts were so bad on my shoulders, legs, and backside that I was ashamed to take my clothes off for physical education class. This was really child abuse. My father did what he thought was best to train me up in the right way. It may not have been right, but I dare to think where I would have ended up if he hadn't put some fear in me. I stay clean today because the whipping that drugs put on me was worse than any punishment my father ever gave me. Relapse is caused most of the time because addicts forget the dope whipping.

The last time my father put his hands on me was the Friday night I was planning to attend our "going over party" after pledging Pershing Rifles for six weeks at Morgan State University in 1966. I was nineteen years old and had played football for a while. The renowned team, coached by Earl Banks, had a forty-six-game winning streak. On this particular night, I pretended to go to bed after fixing Daddy some special tea with something in it to make him go to sleep, but the crushed-up pills did not work. It was getting late, and I got dressed, went downstairs, and proceeded to walk right by my father, who was watching television in the living room. After asking me where I was going, I said a party. His response was no. My response was one of rebellion because this was going to be the party of my life. All my frat brothers would be there, with many females, the special spiked punch, and dancing. I was trying to make my exit when Dad slapped me in the face. My response was, "Don't you ever put your hands on me again." This statement shows that I had gone temporarily insane but didn't realize it until a few minutes later.

My father used to be a boxer. He stood six foot three inches tall and weighed about 260 pounds. He responded by throwing a right to my head. I moved and punched him in the face with my right fist. All the anger of nineteen years of abuse was fueled into that one punch, which knocked him backward, over his easy chair, and onto the floor. My father kept a loaded gun in the bedroom in the drawer or the stand beside his bed. While he lay on the floor, our eyes met for a split second, and I knew that it was time for me to leave home before he got up. I'd seen my father in action with guns, and there was no doubt in my mind that there would have been a Marvin Gaye incident in that living room had I stuck around. I ran out of the house and went to the party. I returned Sunday morning while the family was at church to get my clothes and records. I moved into the frat house, where I lived for about six months with my frat brother, Harold Gordon, until an apartment came through. This preacher's kid had gone wild with wine, women, and song.

Chapter 8

Heroin: Off to the Races and Don't Know It

While moonlighting as a bouncer in a burlesque club, Les Gals, I had the opportunity to meet quite a few people who were considered hustlers. Many of them hung out at an after-hour club known as Cicero's (since closed). The club opened at about two o'clock in the morning, after the bars closed. It cost a dollar to get in, your hand was stamped, food was sold, and you had to buy something to stay in there. The jukebox played the latest rock-and-roll music. You could bring your own alcohol and drink it freely as long as you were orderly.

Anything you wanted was available through the clientele who visited between two and six o'clock in the morning. This is where heroin, known as "boy," entered my life by way of a musician. I'll use the name "Bass," which is not his real name. Bass had a terrible nose habit (snorting heroin) and thought he was being hospitable when he introduced my friend and me to our first blow of heroin. It was considered to be the in thing to sit around and sip on some light wine and snort dope. We didn't know that it was possible for us to get a habit through snorting heroin because we were running off misinformation from people we thought were gurus of the dope culture. The notion that only those who shot dope, intravenous users, could get a habit is a lie that has gotten many innocent people addicted or dead from an overdose.

It was around 1968, and I was selling clothes from the trunk of my 1963 Rambler. The women's clothes were purchased from wholesalers in Manhattan, New York. After I got out of classes at Morgan College, many of my evenings were spent working at the burlesque club and visiting nightspots, selling women's clothing and jewelry. I visited the infamous "Block" where strip clubs were prevalent. I became familiar with the club owners and was allowed to sell my products at the back of the bar or in the owner's office. I had regular clients who purchased clothing and other things that I sold. The women who worked at these places were mainly prostitutes and generally had cash to spend. Sex was constantly offered to me in exchange for my product, but I knew these women were known for "burning" their johns, or customers, with venereal diseases. I said no very quickly because I wanted to stay healthy and knew that having sex with a customer was a sure way of losing a customer and money, too.

Drinking and drugging during working hours was not good business acumen. I needed to be on my toes at all times because I was dealing with people who would rob you quick if they could, or set you up for a scam. However, after work, my road partner and I would head down to Cicero's, count our money, and have some fun. We could buy a cap of dope—a buck pill—for one dollar, and by the time the night was over, we might have snorted two to three pills. The heroin was powerful in those days. Sometimes we bought what was known as "jumbo pills" for two dollars, which came from the eastside of town.

I had to keep moving or the dope would have me in a nod and without full control of my faculties. I remember leaving the after-hour spot alone one night and nodded off at the wheel with my foot on the brake. I woke up about an hour later with my foot still on the brake. I know that it was only by the grace of God that I wasn't robbed or didn't run into something while I was out. There is no question in my mind that it is because of the "prayer cover" of my parents that I am alive today and wasn't killed or didn't overdose on drugs while out there practicing my insanity. I was caught up in the grip of active addiction and did not realize it. Heroin eases up on you like a mouse stealing cheese. It will snap your head off before you know what happened, while you think you're not getting caught like everybody else. This dope, or "boy," would have you thinking the whole world revolves around you and that you are invincible.

Before I left home, I was constantly defying the authority of my parents, especially my father's, who was the undisputed head of the house. There was something inside me that forced me to get out of the house at all cost and stay out past my curfew. Now I know that I was addicted to the lifestyle and was slowly becoming addicted to the drink and drugs. At night I faked sleep and waited until my parents were asleep to sneak out of the house. My bedroom was located on the second floor. I would go through my sister's room and try not to wake her as I opened the window next to her bed. I'd go out on the roof and climbed down the tree. Nightlife, here I come.

Going out the window and down the tree was not so difficult. Coming back up was very dangerous in a drunken condition Many nights I was intoxicated while climbing carefully back up the tree, across the roof, and through the window. As I think back, it had to be the grace and mercy of God that kept me from falling off the roof and breaking my neck, leg, arms, or killing myself. At times my sister would get angry at me for waking her to open the window to let me back in, and she threatened to tell Daddy. But I don't think she ever did. Maybe she might have told once.

There is one night that I will never forget. This was the night I knew my father was off the chain, or I had pushed him almost to the point of no return. I had come home drunk at about three o'clock in the morning. I climbed up the tree to get back in the house, and the window was locked. My sister would not open the window. Frustrated, I crawled back across the slanted roof. I almost fell but caught myself and climbed down the tree. It was a full moon out that night as I knocked on the front screen door, which was locked. The longer I knocked, the louder the knocks and the more upset I became. It was too quiet. Something told me to turn around. There he stood with his silver pistol pointed at me, the light from the moon reflecting off the barrel of the gun. I sobered up immediately, raised my hands, and hollered, "It's me, Daddy, your son. Don't shoot."

My father held the gun steady, still pointed at me. It seemed like he was trying to determine whether he should shoot me anyhow. After a few moments, he finally put the gun down, but I knew somebody was crazy. At the time, I believed it was him. Now I know it was me in deep denial of the addictive state in which I existed. Alcohol and drugs had complete control of my life. However, things progressively got worse.

When a person is caught up in the disease of addiction, it becomes cunning, baffling, and insidious. Cunning is like a snake, sly and crafty. "Baffling" means the addiction is frustrating. The word "insidious" means seductive, gradually, having a cumulative effect. In short, it will have you, and you don't even realize it. By the time you find out that you are caught in the vicious spiral of addiction, it's too late to do anything about it without the help of somebody else. It is almost impossible to become free from the horrors of addiction by yourself. In addition, the disease will talk to you and say, "You can handle it. You can stop anytime you want. Don't tell anybody because if you do, you will blow everything. Keep it to yourself. It's not that bad. You're not as bad as the people who hang on the corner. You can't be an alcoholic because you have a college degree and a job." I was caught up, out of my mind, and didn't have a clue what was going on.

One night while selling clothes out of the trunk of my brand-new1969 Buick, I ran into one of my now-deceased cousins known as Little Man. I was parked on Barkley Street, in front of the bar. My cousin was staying at a friend's house right where I was parked. He didn't want any of the syrup or marijuana I had for sale. Instead, he told me to come upstairs in the house for a treat. We went into the front bedroom and sat on the bed. The light from the streetlight shone through the window. The gas and electric had been turned off. He reached into his pocket, pulled out a syringe and a bag of heroin, and proceeded to cook it up in a soda top. I had never seen anyone shoot dope up close. After he hit himself in the arm, he offered me some. That was the first and last time I ever put a needle in my arm. I was afraid of needles, but because he was my cousin, I let him hit me in the arm, just like he'd done to himself.

There is no doubt in my mind that peer pressure is real, and it is extremely powerful. If you don't have a strong constitution or contact with God, you cannot stand alone for long when your associates are doing what you know is wrong. I didn't even get high because the dope was not powerful enough, he missed my vein, or I was too nervous. I did not want to look like a chump, so I did what he did. There are many people who are dead, in jail, or in mental institutions today because of peer pressure. Learning to say no was a real blessing for me. It developed as a direct result of the many negative consequences I have experienced as the result of saying yes to the wrong things so often. Experience can be a powerful teacher if we learn from our experiences. This is called wisdom. The best way to gain wisdom is by learning from the mistakes of others. This way, some unnecessary pain can be avoided and valuable time gained rather than lost by doing jail time or having a hospital stay.

Even though I had been in church all my life and raised by great parents, there was not a deep, abiding faith living in me. My relationship with the God I heard my father preach about in church was not brought home in an understanding way for me after church was over on Sunday. At least the foundational aspect of having a personal relationship with God was not emphasized. My understanding of Jesus and God was superficial and inexplicable. I guess I was supposed to really learn about Him through the Sunday school classes and Methodist youth fellowship meetings I attended at church. Not until I finally surrendered to my drug addiction, got involved in twelve-step programs like AA and NA did I really begin to understand the God I had heard about all my life. I believe it would have been beneficial if my father had taken some time to teach and discuss the Word of God with me at home. In raising my two children, I spent considerable time teaching them the Bible, praying with them, and interacting with them. Hugging, kissing, and telling them that I love them is very important to me because this is what was lacking in my relationship with my father. It does make a difference in the family relationship when you show love and take time to impart the knowledge of spiritual things.

After pastoring for more than thirty-eight years, I have come to a frightening conclusion. Most people in the traditional church do not know or understand the God they sing, talk, preach, and pray about. This is because the overwhelming majority of religious churchgoers do not study the basic textbook of the church—the Bible. Bible study, if it is held at a church, is attended by approximately 10 to 20 percent of the members, and only about half of these study the lessons or read the Bible regularly. Most people in the church do not mention the Bible in their daily conversations or quote Scripture with book, chapter, and verse. I believe that most religious persons are too intimidated by the world and unfamiliar with the Bible, Koran, or whatever book is foundational to their faith to discuss it intelligently.

Spirituality is much more powerful than religion. Spirituality is lived and springs from the heart. Religion is practiced and comes from the head. In order to overcome active addiction, one must surrender the head to the heart. The head will have us believe that we can quit the destructive behavior anytime we want, but the spirit will cause us to remove self from the equation and allow a Higher Power to take charge. This is where good sponsorship is so powerful. It allows us to be guided by another person who has practiced these spiritual principles. Clean time does not equal recovery. Recovery is determined by how one lives their spiritual principles in daily life.

My third sponsor, who guided me through the steps for about seventeen years, said something to me that I will never forget. One day I asked him why is it that people in NA talk about God more than people in the church? He said, "Basha, the people in church are spending all their time trying to stay out of hell, but we have been to hell and back. We can't help but talk about who saved us!"

I had never participated in a program that was based on me taking a serious, written examination of myself based on tried and proven spiritual principles until becoming a member of a twelve-step program. This was done with the help of an experienced member who had done the same process himself. I think that many of us became addicted because we had no deep roots of a spiritual nature, so we sought a higher power through the flesh, the lower parts of our existence. Alcohol and other drugs become our god and rule our addictive nature by default. It repeats itself time and time again in so many communities, homes, and societies because it requires no real thought or struggle. It's easy to get this negative spirituality anywhere. It comes neatly packaged in a bag, a pill, or a bottle. The real relationship with the true Higher Power costs precious time seeking to find Him, but the reward is beyond measure. It allows the informed, delivered person to know, "I can't, He can, I'll let Him." That's total surrender of mind, body, and soul without a neat package of a powdery substance or a shot glass.

My parents raised me utilizing all the information they had. My mother taught me the traditional prayer, "Now I lay me down to sleep. I pray the Lord my soul to keep. If I should die before I wake. I pray the Lord my soul to take. Amen." My sister and I, at an early age, would kneel beside the bed with Mama between us, fold our hands, and say that prayer. I cannot ever remember my father praying with me or trying to teach me how to pray using Scriptures from the Bible. He prayed over food at every meal and at church events. My father prayed at length on his knees every night before going to bed, and I know that his prayers were genuine, powerful, and effective. However, now being a pastor myself and having the experience of raising my own children, I chose to do it a different way. My mother, now deceased, was a dedicated member of the church I pastored, and I taught her and other believers Spiritual principles that allow them to live disciplined lives *after* I have taught them the Word of God, citing chapter and verse. Effective recovery requires the same type of dedication and study of the basic textbooks written for twelve-step programs.

Since my children were old enough to learn, I taught them how to pray and how to read and study the Bible. My wife and I prayed with them before bed and taught them about the power of prayer. My children and students know the power of prayer and how to pray, and they can teach others the same. We enrolled our children in a Christian preschool called

Kinder Praise, where they learned about Jesus and memorized the names of all sixty-six books in the Bible. My wife, Pia, enrolled them in Awana at the Arlington Baptist Church in Randallstown, Maryland, where they received Christian education and played with other children of various nationalities. I believe if we train our children the right way to live, their lives will be better. Even if they stray, they will come back to the right way because of the teaching at home by loving parents.

Chapter 9

Revelation Knowledge for Family

All good parents and family members want the best for the children. This is especially true for families who raise their children in godly homes and attempt to teach them according to spiritual principles. But it is important to realize that teaching our children spiritual principles, no matter what faith it is, does not exempt them from the possibility of getting into trouble, alcoholism, or drug addiction. My understanding of the principle of training our children righteously implies that there may be a time when they will go astray, but when they get older, they will come back to God's way. The key is that we as parents have planted in them the seeds of faith, hope, and love for God and others. It will take time for those seeds to turn into the harvest for which we yearn. I had to learn this the hard way, through the experiential realities of raising my own children. It's amazing how we can catch amnesia about what we did as children even though we knew better. Parents must be willing to put some things in the hands of the same God who got us through.

Not only did I take my children to church and teach them the Scriptures, I also took them with me to twelve-step meetings for years. They learned about the disease of addiction and how it runs on both sides of my family. They have heard my devastating story of what drugs and alcohol did to me and other family members. My thinking was that my son and daughter would never touch a drink or a drug because of what I put in their heads because addiction begins long before we put the drink or drug in our bodies. The reality is that children have to get their own experiences because they think, *I am smarter than Daddy. It won't happen to me.* We as parents must not try to stand in the way of our children getting what they need to learn. If we do, we get the pain that was not designed for us. Their pain must be felt by them for wisdom to be obtained, if it is ever obtained at all. Pain is a great motivator.

As a practicing licensed drug/alcohol counselor, I have witnessed many parents who were traumatized because they could not stop their children from abusing alcohol or drugs. They tried bribery, manipulation, throwing the drugs away, or other useless means to control the behavior or addiction in the lives of their offspring. At times, I've counseled parents who ended up drinking and drugging with their children or wives or husbands joining their spouses in using drugs in an attempt to get them to stop. Until an individual is ready to surrender to the disease, there is nothing you can do about it but pray and seek professional help. Sometimes an intervention is possible, which can raise the bottom of the addict. But the user must have the desire to stop using, or there will be big trouble on your hands trying to force your family member to stop.

In 1993 I started an Addiction Radio Ministry in Baltimore on WCAO-Heaven 600 AM, which airs on Saturday morning at 7:30 a.m. I interview recovering addicts who tell their story of how they stopped using drinks or drugs. We try to mix up the interviews for all ages in the radio-listening audience to get out our message of hope. My son was about fourteen years old when I asked him to be on air to talk to teens about staying away from drugs. The interview revealed things I never knew were going on in my own neighborhood and his school. The story told by my son really helped me and other parents who were listening. It caused me to reevaluate some of the things I had taken for granted about his knowledge in the area of addiction. Today's teens are privy to many new things at an earlier age than their parents were. Parents need to talk to our children openly and honestly about the realities we know. We also need to listen to them share their ideas and attitudes in private. This enhances the relationship and educational level of parent and child. Parents can think we know everything. We don't. Children can teach us things if we set the stage for learning by intensive listening and open discussion.

It is possible for the disease of addiction to skip a generation, but children have to be very careful when it is already on the family tree. Ask your mom and dad about the history of drug and alcohol use in the family. If your mother, father, brothers, sisters, uncles, or cousins died from using drugs, be honest with them. The truth doesn't need any support. Mr. Shelton, an older member of St. James United Methodist Church in Baltimore, where I used to pastor, used to say, "Every tub has to stand on its own bottom." If our children are going to be affected by the disease of addiction to alcohol or drugs, all we can really do is educate them, pray for them, love them, and leave the rest to God.

At an early age, I was drawn to my father's baby brother, Uncle Harry (now deceased), who was a chauffeur. He would come to visit with his wife, Doll (also deceased). Uncle Harry always had a cigar in one hand and a drink in the other. It was very embarrassing when he always found the bar nearest to where we lived in the town where my dad was the preacher. He would get intoxicated, and there was nothing my dad could do to stop him from drinking. He was the kindest man and always made us laugh. He told my sister, "You always walk like you've got on slippers." I use to think this was so funny as a kid. He owned a large animal farm, gas station, dancehall, restaurant, and boarding house in Virginia called Four Fork Inn. Harry died mysteriously at a young age, about fifty.

I later found out that I had other uncles, on my father's side, who had gotten sidetracked with alcohol, even though all the Jordan boys were great entrepreneurs. Alcohol also took its toll on my mother's father and his brother. There was always alcohol in their homes when we went to visit on holidays. My father didn't like to be around people who drank, and he preached against it. The greatest influence for practicing addicts is another addict who has found recovery and lives the program. There is no better influence than the ripe fruit of recovery that needs no support.

I think my father was an alcoholic who just stopped drinking by the power of God before I was born. He never knew what recovery was, and I got clean eight years after he died in 1980. There is a term for persons who stop drinking but never change the behavior. It's called a dry drunk. hey hMy father had this same self-centered behavior without the alcohol. Daddy was strict on everybody and seldom smiled. He seemed to be angry at the world and was not compassionate. It was hard for me to love my father because I never really felt the love I needed from him. He was always preoccupied with something or someone else. We never hugged, and he never told me that he loved me. The only time my father ever touched me was when he slapped me, whipped my behind, or when we were working or playing around, which was seldom. In raising my children, I regularly tell them, "I love you." I always embrace them and kiss them affectionately. I learned how to do this by being involved in recovery. Everybody needs a hug and wants to hear the words "I love you."

One of the causes for the criminal behavior and incarceration of many young men is the absence of fathers. A father's presence and love are needed just as much as, if not more than, a mother's love. Love is an action word that requires a father to be there when needed. In order to show love, you must possess it and know how to give it away. Fathers are especially needed to head the household and show sons how to be a man first and then how to be a father. The absence of fatherly love in the home causes children to seek love in all the wrong places. Loving fathers show daughters how a husband treats his wife with care and respect, Especially since many daughters marry a man like their fathers. Love is understanding, kind, compassionate, gentle yet firm, and forgiving. Many people use a mind-altering chemical to try to fill a love void. A home where mom and dad are present and exhibit love is a breeding ground for wholesome living and a wholesome family that can be passed down to the next generation. Drugs and alcohol have helped destroy the family value system, especially among African Americans.

Wives need the support of a loving husband, not an abusive, drug-addicted man who didn't have a daddy to teach him about fatherhood. A wife needs a husband to provide legally obtained economic support for the needs of the total household and to help wherever it's needed. If she is constantly chasing the next fix or drink, she cannot properly be the example of a good wife or mother. Her responsibility is to care for the needs of her husband first and then the children. She shows her daughter by example the attributes of a good mother and wife. She also teaches her son the type of woman he should seek for a wife and mother to his children. Sons often marry a woman just like mom. There needs to be godlier mothers and fathers in the "village" who are surrogate parents to those who have none. When mom and dad are drug- and alcohol-free, this carries a tremendous message to children alive and yet unborn. This positive family legacy is needed to change the tide of our babies being born and raised as fuel for incarceration, mental institutions, welfare, and early death. The loving family is the seed for a positive work ethic, moral values, and successful men and women.

My grandfather, Elder Jordan Sr., was a slave. He received his emancipation at the age of fifteen and went on to build a great legacy in Florida through land acquisition and investments. The name Jordan came from a white slave master in or around Clearwater, Florida, where my father was born. I can imagine how my father was raised. Men didn't cry or show emotion at that time. My grandfather probably raised his five sons like the slave master raised him. We are products of our environment and heredity. It is extremely difficult to get away from either one. Alcohol was quite prevalent back during those years, and many made their own wine and corn liquor at home. I don't know about my grandfather's use of alcohol, but my uncle, Elder Jr., who died at age ninety-four, ran a few bars, two beaches, and a nightclub in St. Petersburg, Florida. He built the historical Manhattan Casino on Twenty-second Street South, which showcased Duke Ellington, Count Basie, Fats Domino, and other famous artists. My uncle Elder was a well-known, wealthy, businessman who also operated the first bus line between Tampa and St. Pete although alcohol played an important part in his life.

It is only by the grace of God, my parents' prayers, and my wife's determination to help me that I am who I am today. The strong family values instilled in my father by his parents and my mother's grandmother had a lot to do with the success of my parents and me. Like my son says, "Family means everything." Add to that a strong constitution, trust in God, a good education, and staying sober will propel you to greatness. Nothing is impossible when you have a loving family to support you, stay clean one day at a time, and stay focused on where you are going.

Chapter 10

The Pipe

Normally, a person doesn't just pick up cocaine and use it. He or she is introduced to it through a family member, friend, or acquaintance. One night in 1974, while selling women's clothing out of the trunk of my late-model Cadillac Coupe de-Ville, a casual friend of mine (I'll use the name Joe) sold me a spoon of cocaine for $60. He claimed I could make a lot of money selling it. Since I knew he was a hustler who made a lot of money, I believed him. I snorted a small bit of it but didn't get high. Joe was known for being ruthless, trigger-happy, and a hothead, so I proceeded with caution in asking him for a refund. At first he tried to make excuses and told me that I didn't know what I had. He eventually took it back, and we became closer because of how I approached him. Little did he know that I was prepared to shoot him first if he had given me the slightest indication that he was going for his gun. Thank God it worked out because I really didn't want to hurt him.

"Association breeds assimilation," my daddy use to say. The only reason I carried a gun was because the men I hung with carried guns. Peer pressure had me doing things just to be accepted by my evil associates. The level of excitement that I felt by doing wrong did not quiet the voices of my parents and the positive teachings imbedded within—even though I ignored the voices much of the time. Some thirty years later, Joe and I met up again. He had gone to prison and on his release, got saved in the church and put the old life behind him. Our paths crossed at an NA meeting, and Joe was a guest on my recovery radio broadcast. He carried a powerful message of recovery because of his experiences, strengths, and hope. He is one of the few people still living who was in the old circle of gangsters with whom I ran. We are not only blessed to be alive and drug-free but grateful for being spared while others are dead or in prison after doing the same things we did. We are chosen along with countless others who found a new way of living.

I really didn't know what I had or how to use it correctly when Joe sold me that spoon of cocaine. Later, I found out that what he had sold me was more potent than I realized. Cocaine was not in my story until some years later. However, I did have a short run with some pink powder called "monster," which was similar to cocaine. Monster was my forerunner to cocaine because it prepared my mind, body, soul, and nose for coke, called the "white girl."

A friend who was a notorious heroin dealer in east Baltimore showed me how to cut pure heroin and make some fast money. We decided to go to the Penn Relays and have some fun. During the trip we stopped by his aunt's house just to say hello. She kept her dope in a hatbox, and she was the one who introduced me to monster. It was a high, like cocaine, but had a lot of speed in it. There were about seven of us who rode together to Philly. Coming back to Baltimore, the monster had me so disoriented, I got lost driving around the expressway for two hours. Monster causes you to stay awake for days and become very jittery. I had to eventually leave it alone because it made me feel too uncomfortable. We were armed and dangerous enough; I didn't need to be paranoid with a pistol.

Be careful what you say you will never do again. The year was 1980, and I had graduated from Wesley Theological Seminary in Washington DC in May. My father died in September, and I was going through a divorce. I had left a student pastoral appointment in western Maryland and was now senior pastor of my first full-time church as a United Methodist minister. There was a tremendous amount of stress, and marijuana was a regular friend and companion. I was going back and forth to Baltimore to check on some rental property and see my mother. Hennessey and Johnny Walker were really good road partners along with Coors Light beer. Though smoking cigarettes, I jogged four to five miles regularly and exercised at least three days a week to stay in shape.

Trying to live holy while only reading the Bible when it was time to prepare sermons on Saturday night was difficult, especially being single again after a painful divorce. Beautiful church sisters trying to get to the man of God was trying to my faith. Older women put their daughters and granddaughters up to marry the pastor through tasty meals and other means. My prayer life was shallow. I didn't know then the real importance of having a daily walk with God through the Word and concentrated fasting and prayer.

Unknowingly, my soul was wide open for the Enemy to grip me through my own ignorance of addiction. That's when cocaine came on the scene in a different way than snorting. The pipe entered the pulpit. The beginning of the end was present without my knowledge or permission. Ignorance is not only powerful; it will get you a prison cell, institutionalized, or a pine box unless a miracle happens. You cannot escape the horrors of addiction on your own. I tried it many times and failed, miserably. Please do not take this statement lightly. You cannot escape the horrors of addiction on your own. We need somebody or something outside ourselves to help us when we cannot help ourselves. You can take that truth to the bank and cash it in.

Whoever you are, don't be fooled by pointing at me and saying I should have known better. I did know better than to try something that is illegal and has a reputation of killing human beings. But I thought it would never happen to me because of who I was. What I didn't know about cocaine, alcohol, and other drugs almost killed me. The same can happen to you. If you don't believe me, you're in for a very rude awakening—if you live. I hope and pray that this statement got your attention. The purpose of this book is to educate readers about the addictive powers of drugs and alcohol. Addiction doesn't care who you are, what your educational background is, who your family is, where you come from, or where you think you are going. Addiction will change your life without your permission. We are powerless over people, places, and things. They don't always do what we want them to do. My sincere prayer is that you and members of your family don't have to go through the pain of active addiction because you think you can handle it. I thought I could handle alcohol, cocaine, and other drugs, but I couldn't. This revelation came, unfortunately, after many failed attempts to quit. I would rather you pretend to believe me than to try smoking cocaine or any other drug, get the pain, and then realize that I am right.

Peer pressure is a tremendous hurdle to overcome, even as an adult. I went to visit a fraternity brother who has since died. We became close while attending college, and we both liked to smoke marijuana. It was as common to us as lighting up a cigarette when we were together. We were relaxing in his plush sitting room, smoking a joint, when the doorbell rang. He had some company and told me he would be right back. I sat there but eventually got tired of waiting. So I went into the kitchen. They were all gathered in a circle around the stove, passing a pipe. I figured this must be the cocaine being smoked rather than snorted I'd heard about. When the pipe came in my direction, I took it, did what they did, inhaled, and immediately fell in love with the so-called the white girl. This was the beginning of the end. The pipe was now in charge of my life. It became my higher power. The God I'd known all my life was now in second place. I immediately began to live to use and used to live. My world revolved around an expensive white powder that had extraordinary power in every area of my life.

It is possible to have too much money, and if you suffer from the disease of addiction, your money will mysteriously disappear. Between alcohol, cocaine, marijuana, and cigarettes, hundreds of dollars vanished on a weekly basis. My salary as a pastor was not bad, but this, in addition to other investments, allowed my financial sense to become way off balance. The time spent at home with my wife and toddler son became less and less as well. Something had to change. Something was wrong, but a workable plan was not in sight. I constantly told myself I could stop anytime I wanted, but that only lasted a few days. Then I had to celebrate and was off to the races again, using uncontrollably.

The money I spent while smoking cocaine was ridiculous, but I could not help myself. A friend told me that if I just snorted the coke instead of smoking the pipe, I'd be better off and wouldn't get a habit. His advice sounded good, so I tried it. The pipe was put down, and I began to only snort the coke. Occasionally, I put some in a joint of reefer. The result was no different than the pipe. My use was uncontrollable. I was caught up and didn't know how to stop permanently. Many times I thought about suicide and put myself in situations where death would be near. But God had another plan for my life, I can recall nine times the death angel was so near that I could feel him, see him, and smell him. The death angel I've seen is a dirty shade of gray and a familiar spirit to me.

Crack cocaine, which is prevalent on the streets of every major US city today, has been processed, so it costs less than powered cocaine. It causes your brain and thinking patterns to become irrational. Smoking and snorting cocaine allowed me to experience something worse than death because death was a welcomed visitor when he came. The problem was that death did not stay and finish the job of killing me as my disease wanted. Some stop using drugs because of the fear of dying. I will not use a drug ever again because of my tormenting experience of wanting to die, but God would not let me die!

Drugs, alcohol and cigarettes are disproportionately advertised and distributed in the African American communities of America because of the latent belief of superiority of many whites. Also, it is a systematic means whereby African Americans are disproportionately arrested, imprisoned, and killed by police. It is one of the new covert, means of slavery, jim-crow and discrimination employed by the majority. The results are apathy, increased mental disorder and deaths in child birth, This also affects underemployment, decreased levels of educational achievement and lower levels of poverty. The solution is Spiritual in nature which allows recovery to then become possible . The conditions of the entire community change and the attitudes of the people are resurrected from dope to hope.

Death cannot take what God has in His hands. My desire to die rather than continue using drugs is a feeling I will never forget, along with the gratitude I have for how and what my Higher Power has done in my life. Had I not had my valley of the shadow of death experience and God's rescue, my ministry, Hope Alive Outreach, Inc., would not be so powerful. My thirty years of active addiction and almost thirty years in recovery have prepared me to be a living vessel and example of what God can and will do. I am hope alive! I live hope, breathe hope, and preach, teach, and resonate hope. I give Jesus Christ all the honor and praise for what He has, is, and will do through my resurrected life. I'm just like Jesus. I've died to drugs and been resurrected to a new life in the kingdom of God. There is plenty of room here for many more who want freedom from active addiction; you just have to ask. Thank God I got it to give and don't mind sharing the hope, not the dope.

Chapter 11

The Pulpit

When God called me to preach, I was about twenty years old. Being a pastor was the farthest thing from my mind. However, after running from the ministry for seven years, I finally surrendered, quit the clothing business, and went to Wesley Theological Seminary in Washington DC. After being in seminary for a year, in 1977 I was appointed to a student charge for three years. Someone has said that God protects babies and fools. He definitely protected me as I made several blunders as a young preacher. My addiction was brewing without my knowledge while the church grew, especially after my first wife and I broke up. I learned the hard way that alcohol and drugs cloud the message from the pulpit. Some things are learned only by making mistakes and getting older. It's called getting wisdom.

Drinking with families after funerals and partying with a select few may be fun for a while, but it ruins your character and reputation. Just because there was numerical growth did not mean there was spiritual growth in the church. After a while, it became increasingly difficult to minister with all the gossip and contradictions in my life. I prayed and vowed to God that if He got me out of this situation, I would never behave the same way again, especially with the women. He got me out of that church, and I have kept my promise to the Lord ever since that day.

I graduated from seminary in May of 1980 and was appointed to my first full-time church. It was a rural atmosphere with a closely knit community, and I was determined to be the best pastor possible. Whenever I wanted to relax and indulge, I went to Baltimore or somewhere away from my members. Things went well until I got engaged to the former pastor's daughter instead of one of the many fine young ladies in the church. We got married, attendance dropped immediately, and many attitudes changed despite the positive relationships that had been established. The United Methodist Church decided that my services were better suited in my hometown of Baltimore. I never wanted to pastor in Baltimore because I had too much negative history there.

Nevertheless, in 1983 we moved to Baltimore, and my addiction took off.

The pipe and the pulpit caused spiritual warfare personified. There was hardly a day that I didn't use some form of drug or alcohol to ease the pain. Little did I realize that addiction is obsessive-compulsive behavior and progressive. The more I drank, the more I needed to cover the void in my life. I realize now that the void was spiritual in nature as I was living against God's will. Using cocaine or marijuana became horrible. Preaching became a chore because of the inner turmoil. I spent considerable time ministering to others through drug seminars at the church and visiting elementary schools, speaking to the children about drug prevention. I guess I was trying to help myself through helping others. However, there were times when I stayed out all night on Saturday and had to call someone else to preach for me on Sunday morning because I was caught up in the grip of active addiction. Smoking coke had become my higher power, my God.

Trying to hide my addiction from others was a major task, and it was killing me on the inside. I wanted help but did not know how to get it. My wife arranged for me to see a counselor, who was an Episcopal priest, and even made an appointment for me to enter outpatient treatment. I went to the facility but left abruptly because of the fear of being exposed and not knowing how to live without a drink or drug. Fear had me stuck.

One of the most embarrassing situations happened to me one night when I was at the home of my cocaine supplier, waiting for his supplier to arrive. We were upstairs in his entertainment area, smoking herb and drinking Hennessey, when the doorbell rang. I usually went into the bathroom when company came and stayed until they left, especially if I didn't know them. However, this time I remained where I was because he left the cocaine on the table for me to use freely. This treat did not happen often, so I took my chances. Three people—two women and a man—came upstairs with him and sat down. As we sat there, getting high together, the brother kept starring at me. He finally snapped his fingers and said, "Now I know who you are. You're the pastor of the church downtown! How do you do that?"

I responded by snorting some more cocaine and said, "That's how I do it. How do you do it?" It got real quiet in the room. My heart was in my mouth, and I wished I had gone to the bathroom. My sin was found out. I got up and left, broken, hurt, but trying to appear strong. Some things that God brought me through I will never forget. Things like this help keep me clean today. Relapse occurs when we forget the pain but remember the pleasure. Everything that's good to you is not good for you.

My prayers constantly asked God for help, but He was taking too long to come through in a way that was acceptable to me. Sometimes I went before the altar early Sunday morning after being out all night. I lay prostrate, crying and begging God to release me from this terrible way of life. Little did I know He was working it out without my help in a way that only the Higher Power can do. I know now that prayer works in any situation for anyone who is sincere. Be careful what you pray for because it may be answered and catch you unprepared.

> Ask and it shall be given you, seek and you shall find; knock and it shall be opened unto you. (Matthew 7:7 KJV)

One of the greatest assets I learned by ministering to others while experiencing tribulation and pain is the power of prayer. It is a very sad preacher who does not know how to pray or the benefits of prayer no matter what is happening around him or her. I would pray for others, and it seemed like God cared for them more than He cared for me. Faith and prayer go together. My prayers for my own deliverance never stopped, no matter how angry I got at God. I knew deep down inside He was either going to answer my prayer, or I was going to die believing and praying for relief. Most of my sermons the last couple of years before I got clean were really cries for God to give hope to the hopeless. I preached from biblical texts about Jesus delivering people who could not make it without Him. I was hopeless, broken, and sick and tired of living that way. The pulpit was my place to cry out for help and hope for anyone who would listen, especially me.

I wanted God to prove He would do it for me, too. There were many who got saved through hearing my messages at the end of my active addiction and right after my deliverance. My sincerity and longing for relief and hope had to be felt because it was real. Real pulpiteers are felt in the pews. Identification takes place, and the pew knows the pulpit is speaking heartfelt, passionate, truth. My gratitude, even today, is felt by hearers because it is filled with the hope for which I so desperately prayed. My life today is a traveling pulpit of hope because I am eternally grateful that God finally answered my prayer. This flame of gratitude will never change. I know what a joy it is today to possess the hope I had lost. That's why all the ministries I have founded begin with hope: Hope Alive Ministry, Hope Alive Ministry Deliverance Fellowship (the church), The House of Hope (men's recovery house), Hope Alive Outreach, and Hooked on Hope (radio broadcast).

One of my friends who graduated with me from Baltimore City College High School in 1965 is now one of the greatest preachers in America. Reverend Doctor Charles Booth pastors a church in Ohio. I invited him to preach a revival for me at St. James United Methodist Church in September of 1988.The final night he preached on the subject "Why David Couldn't Fly." He used the following text.

> My heart is sore pained within me: and the terrors of death are fallen upon me. Fearfulness and trembling are come upon me, and horror hath overwhelmed me. And I said, Oh that I had wings like a dove! For then would I fly away, and be at rest. (Psalm 55:4–6 KJV)

That night was a major turning point in my life. While he preached the power and glory of God fell on the house. First, the sound system went out, but he kept on preaching. The lights went out, and he kept on preaching. Thank God we had emergency lights that came on. I knew he was preaching to me because his description of King Davidwho wrote the psalm, was exactly how I felt. As I sat in the pulpit, an inner transformation took place, and I knew something was up. Then Dr. Booth jumped from the pulpit over the altar like an eagle, flying. It was miraculous and supernatural to see. He said, "There is somebody here tonight who is just like David and needs to come to the altar to be cleansed and healed." That person was me. Broken, fearful, and overwhelmed, I got up and was the first one at the altar. I stretched myself out on the floor, facedown, crying unto the Lord. That was September 5, 1988, the last day I used cocaine.

If you want your life to be changed, keep on praying, keep on going to church, and hear the Word from a passionate preacher. Your faith will come by hearing the Word of God. I know because it happened to me. It can happen to you, too!

Whenever you're going through something you cannot handle, God will send somebody to open the door for your escape. Even though I stopped using cocaine, I didn't realize that alcohol was a drug. My drinking escalated to the point that my wife became greatly irritated when she saw beer and wine in the refrigerator. She hated alcohol and what it was doing to me. Our relationship was very strained due to my insane behavior and my threats to kill her if she told anyone about my drinking and drugging. I was totally unaware of what she had initiated behind the scenes. Thank God for a faithful, determined, God-fearing wife who practices the sacred vows we shared in the service of matrimony: "To love, honor, and keep each other in sickness and in health, until death us do part."

I was not only her husband but her pastor as well. This ordeal was putting a tremendous strain on her respect and trust in me. I love her more today than ever before because of her steadfast love for me, not just through my addiction, but today in my deliverance. Thank God for my wife.

There are pastors in the pulpit today who need the prayers of the people because it is no easy job preaching, teaching, and living the Word we preach. There will always be more struggle in the pulpit than in the pew because Satan does not want the shepherd to get the message of hope and salvation to the sheep. We also need to pray daily for ourselves. If you need help facing your addiction, God has called me and anointed me to give you hope. You can call me at 443-250-9635 for guidance in deliverance, marriage counseling, and treatment information. Or e-mail me at ProphetBasha@aol.com. Our website is www.HopeAliveMinistry.org. The mailing address is P. O. Box 35427, St. Petersburg FL 33712. There are numerous videos on YouTube from Hope Alive Outreach that can educate you about addiction.

God has a plan for all His people, especially pastors and those in the fivefold ministry (Ephesians 4:11–12ff KJV). The deeper God has to reach to bring us out of addiction or sin, the higher He will take us in the kingdom as we do His will. It took a twelve-step program for me to find out who I was in Christ and to begin to understand the God I'd preached about for eleven years. Until I got delivered, the ministry was a job. Now it is a life. The pulpit before deliverance was a place to shine and be seen, but now it is a sacred, chosen place to be transparent enough to give the hope I have to others who struggle with any addiction. Always remember that no matter what you are going through, there is hope for you. The Higher Power who rules this universe has great plans for you, but the drugs have to go, or you will go to jail or institution, or die. Choose hope brothers and sisters, especially if you stand in the pulpit.

Chapter 12

The Intervention: Free at Last

Living in a drug-infested neighborhood in Baltimore's inner city, next to the church I pastored, compelled me to move my family to the suburbs for the safety of our son, Basha III, and where I could raise horses. I had purchased a retired thoroughbred racehorse named Cosmelia from the Rocking R Ranch in Randallstown, Maryland. On Friday, October 13, 1988, I sat at my kitchen table, making arrangements with a contractor to install fencing around my farm so I could bring Cosmelia home, when there was a knock at the door. It was 9 a.m. Who could be coming at this time of the morning without notice? As I opened the door, there stood my mother and my sister. I invited them in, but before I could close the door, in came my best friend, Rev. Milton King; my mother-in-law, Louise Winters; my district superintendent; and the Episcopal priest who had been counseling me. The priest told the contractor he had to leave. I became upset but knew something big was about to happen. My wife had been instrumental in orchestrating an intervention for me with the help of the priest. I was instructed to go into the living room and listen to what each person had to say.

As the intervention unfolded, each person proceeded to tell me of a time when they had observed my addictive behavior. Each one ended with the same statement: "Basha, if you do the right thing, everything will be all right."

I finally asked, "What is the right thing."

The priest, Dr. Michael Rokos, answered, "Basha, you have to go into treatment today."

I said, "I can't go today because I have to get this fencing installed. I can go later." Then I was informed that Bishop Joseph Yeakel had been informed about what was going on. I jumped up so high I almost hit the ceiling. "What?" I shouted, and I began to cry. A tremendous burden was immediately lifted from me because I knew God had answered my prayer. I felt free at last.

To be able to stop hiding and acting like nothing was going on was a tremendous emotional weight lifted from my total being. Freedom. The feeling was similar to the way I felt when released from city jail in 1969 after spending thirty days behind bars for a crime I didn't commit. Freedom. I was so glad to be released that I walked from downtown to Morgan Park, about seven miles. It reminds me of a song we used to sing in a little, country church my father pastored in Calvert County, Maryland: "Nobody knows the trouble I've seen; nobody knows my sorrow. Nobody knows but Jesus." Glory hallelujah! Carrying the weight of emotional guilt and shame for three decades but now being set free was a miracle. Now I had to learn that freedom isn't free. It costs you everything if you want to keep it.

My wife had packed my bags with new clothes for me to attend a thirty-day treatment facility, Hidden Brook, in Bel Air, Maryland (now closed). My best friend drove me there, which was located in a serene, wooded atmosphere surrounded by farmland. On arrival, I was escorted to a shared room and then taken to another room for an interview. A nurse walked me to the interview room. She put her arm around me and said, "You have to forgive yourself. God has already forgiven you. You are not a bad person. You suffer from the disease of addiction. You will be all right." I put my head on her shoulder and cried. These were tears of joy and happiness. I had never cried like that in public all my life. This nurse must have been an angel in disguise. She said all I needed to do was be willing to let go and let God do whatever He had to do for my deliverance. I have done this daily since Friday, October 13, 1988.

God answers prayer for real, for real. But He doesn't answer them in our time or the way we expect. Sometimes we need to be humiliated before we get to the point of surrender to a Higher Authority who knows more than we know. The famous last words of addicts are, "I know." If I knew so much, why did I suffer so long? To show my gratitude for what He has done for me, I constantly find ways to freely give back what was so freely given to me. I'm free at last and need to find another suffering addict to share the hope given to me!

I waited patiently for the Lord, and He inclined unto me and heard my cry. He brought me up also out of a horrible pit, out of the miry clay, and set my feet upon a rock and established my goings (Psalm 40:1–2 KJV).

The beginning of my deliverance had come finally come. During the twenty-eight days at the treatment facility, I learned about the disease of addiction and how to stay clean, one day at a time, by living certain spiritual principles in my life on a daily basis. On coming out of treatment, I was blessed to be put in contact with my first sponsor by a counselor at the treatment center who became a good friend until his death.

During these twenty-seven years of recovery, I've had four sponsors and five pastors who have had great influence in my life and ministry. Bishop Anthony Muse, founder/pastor of Ark of Safety Christian Church in Oxen Hill, Maryland, gave me spiritual support and $5,000 dollars to start Hope Alive Ministry Deliverance Fellowship. The late Dr. Harold Carter Sr. pastor of New Shiloh Baptist Church in Baltimore, was there to listen to and counsel me when other pastors turned their backs on me. Bishop Don Meares, pastor of Evangel Cathedral in Upper Marlboro, Maryland, showed me the value of having a spiritual covering and was there for me whenever I needed him. Bishop Roger Tatuem, pastor and founder of Helping Hands Ministries in Churchville, Maryland, has been a confidant and friend since 1958. Finally, Apostle Leroy Thompson, Sr., pastor of Ever Increasing Word Ministries in Darrow, Louisiana, is my spiritual father who has catapulted me into the realm of supernatural prosperity (Money Cometh) through his teaching on sowing, faith, and grace.

Chapter 13

There Is Hope for You

All of us have innate qualities that have been with us since birth. It is our job to find out what these qualities or gifts are. Once we tap into these gifts, life is on and popping. My daddy always told me that I had to do more and be more than he did. This was encouragement from home and from the most important man in my life at the time—my father. I felt I could do anything. I began selling things through mail order at the age of ten or eleven. Thus began a life as a self-starter and an entrepreneur. My dad stimulated something inside me that I did not know was there.

This book is written to ignite a spark of hope, of greatness, in you that you never knew existed. Please don't let my desire for greatness in you be more than the desire you have for greatness in yourself. Take some time to write down your dreams for yourself, no matter how far-fetched they may be or what others think. Put your mind on things above and beyond where you are now. Create a simple plan to learn all you can about your dream position or accomplishments. Educate yourself, go back to school, ask someone who has faith in you to help you. God will put people in your life to assist you to get where He designed you to go. Don't allow a drink or a drug to stop you from your positive destiny. Put concrete hope in your veins rather than temporary dope, which will detour you from your positive gains.

One night I was standing at the door of Les Gals as the bouncer, and a young man came in and sold me a ring. He convinced me that I could do what he did and make a lot of money. I believed him. We eventually became friends, and he turned me on to his jewelry and clothing suppliers in Baltimore and New York. My gifts of gab and sales took off, and I became a successful businessman. When I became a minister, I learned about faith in God and in my own abilities. Somehow I adopted this Scripture on faith, and it has been my marching theme for ministry and life since 1988: "Now faith is the substance of things hoped for, the evidence of things not seen" (Hebrews 11:1 KJV).

I never lost my faith, and by keeping faith, hope showed up again when I lost sight of God. It is possible to think that we're all alone and God has gone. But if you're still alive, He's there, too, carrying us when we are running on self-will and blind, trying to handle life all alone.

There was a time in my life when I lost all hope and thought that God had abandoned me. Death, to me, would have been a welcome visitor. Now I realize that the times when I was most distraught, He was there all the time. The faith that my parents instilled in me never died, even though I wanted to die. God had another plan for me. If I had never been exposed to the horrors of addiction and the joys of deliverance/recovery, I would not be in the position to show others there is hope beyond addiction. Hope Alive Ministry Deliverance Fellowship, The House of Hope, Hope Alive Outreach, and the Recovery Radio broadcast would have never been created if God didn't have an assignment for me to carry out in the earth's realm for Him. He also has an assignment for you. Don't try to overcome your addiction alone. Call a professional for whatever plagues you. Call me at 443-250-9635, or write me at Hope Alive Outreach, P.O. Box 35427, St. Petersburg, FL. You can also e-mail me at ProphetBasha@aol.com or check out our website at www.HopeAliveMinistry.org.

When I look back over my journey through addiction, I realize it was my Higher Power who orchestrated my life and protected me, "through the valley of the shadow of death" (Psalm 23:4 KJV). One weekend when I was in college, I went to a Pershing Rifle fraternity picnic, and my canoe turned over in the Back River. Thank God I had on a life jacket. The water was dirty, cloudy, and deep. It took a power greater than myself to spare my life in those murky waters for an hour and a half before my frat brothers, Harold Gordon and Melvin Butler, saved me.

When I was high from drugs and alcohol in 1968 at the Mt. Royal Amusement Center and getting beaten up by an underworld associate, it was God who had the police come cruising by just in the nick of time to save me. It had to be the Higher Power that caused my assailant to leave before I came back with my father's gun to kill him. Drugs cause temporary insanity. Today, he and I are both ministers. He is an imam, and I am a prophet. Never lose faith just because you can't see or understand everything. Keep praying no matter what happens, and God will show up in a way you don't expect. It's the evidence of things not seen.

On putting my life on rewind, I know it was His hand that saved me one night outside the afterhours club Cicero's when the police raided the street as I got in the front seat of my friend's car. The doorman, who was selling coke, was getting into the backseat when the police ran down on us. Guns drawn, one policeman had a bead on the driver at the front left bumper, and another policeman had a gun pointed eight inches from my face. In order for the doorman to get in the backseat, I had to lean forward and pull up the backseat with my right hand. When I looked up, there was this gun in my face, and the man behind it saying, "Don't move, or I'll kill you." His hand was shaking; the hammer was cocked.

I was scared to death, looking down the barrel of that .38 revolver and quietly said, "I won't move. Please don't shoot me." You talk about being still and knowing that God is God (Psalm 46:10 KJV). I was as still as a picture and know that it was only by the grace of God that I came through this.

Addiction will make you crazy, and you are the last one to find it out. I was supposed to graduate from Morgan University in 1969 but got into an altercation that pushed my graduation back to 1970. Around January of 1969, I found myself with several other ungodly men going to a party. We stopped by a house on Calvert Street before the party to get high. Somehow we began to play cops and robbers with loaded guns, pretending we were shooting each other as we hid like little kids. Finally, as we were leaving, a friend and I were walking across the street when a car almost hit us, and the white passengers called us a name that lit a fuse of anger! Then gunshots were fired at the speeding car from behind us as my friends had seen what happened. Three of us jumped in my car and were in hot pursuit. I ran a red light and ran their car over almost on the sidewalk.

With guns drawn, I proceeded to lay out these three men who were sitting about three feet away. I was enraged when one of them pulled a shotgun on us from the backseat of their car. A shot was fired from the backseat of my car, which scared me terribly. I put my gun down and stepped on the gas. They got out of the car to fire on us, but little did they know that my friends in a convertible were coming behind them. Two people got shot, but we didn't know it, so we proceeded to the party. We made a stop on Ensor Street when the police came down on us like gangbusters.

Fifteen to twenty cars must have surrounded us. One officer had a megaphone and said, "Get out the car and don't move," *How do you do that? I thought. I have to move to get out of the car.* As we opened the doors and got out, a frightening sound pierced the air. It was the distinct sound of guns being cocked, ready to kill. We knew if one officer fired on us, all would fire.

It is good to remember where you have come from and at times relive your trying journey. It will help you avoid relapse. I know my Redeemer lives, moves, and watches over me. If you give yourself a break and stop using just for today, He will work it out if you surrender, pray, and keep the faith.

I am a grateful, recovering, delivered addict who is eternally thankful for where He has brought me from, where I am now, and where He is taking me. I am a witness that God can raise you from a pit to a plateau, from the pipe to a life-changing pulpit that is incomprehensible if we turn our wills and our lives over to Him. And remember, no matter what's going on with you today, there is hope for you.